101 Th n
Arkansas
Before You Die

Books by Kat Robinson

Arkansas Pie:
A Delicious Slice of the Natural State
History Press, 2012

Classic Eateries of the Ozarks
and Arkansas River Valley
History Press, 2013

Classic Eateries of the Arkansas Delta
History Press, 2014

Another Slice of Arkansas Pie:
A Guide to the Best Restaurants, Bakeries,
Truck Stops and Food Trucks
for Delectable Bites in The Natural State
Tonti Press, 2018

Arkansas Food:
The A to Z of Eating in The Natural State
Tonti Press, 2018

101 Things to Eat in Arkansas Before You Die
Tonti Press, 2019

102 More Things to Eat in Arkansas
Before You Die
Tonti Press, 2019

43 Tables:
An Internet Community Cooks During Quarantine
Tonti Press, 2020

A Bite of Arkansas:
A Cookbook of Natural State Delights
Tonti Press, 2020

And coming soon:
The Arkansas Church and Community
Cookbook Collection, Volume 1
Tonti Press, 2021

101 Things to Eat in
Arkansas
Before You Die

A Travel Guide to the Very Best
Plates in The Natural State

Kat Robinson

TONTI
PRESS

Published by Tonti Press
Little Rock, Arkansas

Cover image of the chicken and catfish dinner plate with sour cream potatoes, tartar sauce, green tomato relish, hush puppies, homemade bread, butter, tea and Grapette taken at Woods Place in Camden.

Back cover illustration by the author.

All photography by Kat Robinson except pages 22 (Kopper Kettle Smokehouse), 31 (Ozark Café), and 36 (Wiederkehr Weinkeller), all by Grav Weldon, with permission.

First published August 2019
Second printing December 2020

Manufactured in the United States of America

ISBN 13: 978-0-9998734-5-8

Library of Congress Control Number: 2019947279

No restaurant, bakery, store or other entity paid for inclusion within these pages. All food photography was taken without manipulation, augmentation or exaggeration. Every food item is edible and as would be served in each establishment. The author received no monetary compensation to insert, rank, or exclude any property in this list.

EATER,
Prepare to dine.

TABLE OF CONTENTS

I've eaten all over Arkansas, as a food historian, as a food writer, and even as a citizen of this state. There are far too many fantastic restaurants to properly determine which is the absolute best. However, I'm often asked for the "best places in Arkansas" by folks both within and without our borders. The selection of these restaurants was tedious, burdensome and absolutely heartbreaking. Trying to narrow down our spectrum of options to a mere 101 locations proved to be extraordinarily difficult.

These restaurants contained within this book can be considered some of the best we have. You'll find a lot of classics in these pages, and a few younger restaurants, too. Like the people who live here, these eateries cross social strata, region, price point and cuisine. Each and every one is worthy.

Feel free to use the handy list and checkbox at the front of each section for noting which eateries you have visited. The color edge corresponds to the map denoting these dining regions.

Enjoy.

NORTHWEST

- [ ] A.Q. Chicken House, Springdale
- [ ] Benson's Grill, Fort Smith
- [ ] Calico County, Fort Smith
- [ ] Catfish Hole, Alma/Fayetteville
- [ ] Cliff House Inn, Jasper
- [ ] DeVito's Restaurant, Bear Creek Springs
- [ ] Ed Walker's Drive In, Fort Smith
- [ ] Ermilio's Italian Home Cooking, Eureka Springs
- [ ] Feltner's Whatta-Burger, Russellville
- [ ] Grandma's House Café, Winslow
- [ ] Hammontree's Grilled Cheese, Fayetteville/Rogers
- [ ] Herman's Ribhouse, Fayetteville
- [ ] Kopper Kettle Smokehouse, Van Buren
- [ ] Local Flavor Café, Eureka Springs
- [ ] Low Gap Café, near Jasper
- [ ] Martin Greer's Candies, Gateway
- [ ] Monte Ne Inn Chicken Restaurant, Monte Ne
- [ ] Neal's Café, Springdale
- [ ] Neighbor's Mill, Harrison/Rogers
- [ ] Oark General Store, Oark
- [ ] The Old South, Russellville
- [ ] Ozark Café, Jasper
- [ ] Taliano's Italian Restaurant, Fort Smith
- [ ] The Hive at 21c Museum Hotel, Bentonville
- [ ] Tusk and Trotter, Bentonville
- [ ] The Venesian Inn, Tontitown
- [ ] Wiederkehr Weinkeller, Wiederkehr Village
- [ ] The Wooden Spoon, Gentry

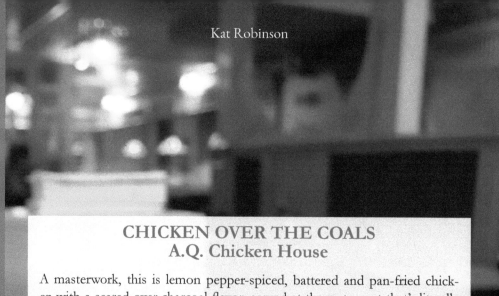

CHICKEN OVER THE COALS
A.Q. Chicken House

A masterwork, this is lemon pepper-spiced, battered and pan-fried chicken with a seared-over-charcoal flavor, served at the restaurant that's literally named "Arkansas Quality." A traditional three piece chicken dinner comes with two sides; the seasoning is also available on wings and tenders. Be sure to get some of the famed rolls to enjoy with butter and honey before your entree arrives.

1207 North Thompson Street (U.S. Highway 71B), Springdale
(479) 751-4633 * AQChickenHouse.net

ARKANSAS FOOD HALL·FAME
FINALIST

10

MOUNT CHILIMANJARO
Benson's Grill

The ultimate open-faced chili cheeseburger, this is Benson's Grill's prime burger patty on an open bun covered in housemade chili, shredded Cheddar cheese, chopped red onion and crinkle cut dill pickle slices, served with potato chips - a summit of epic diner food available 24 hours a day. The sweet potato pancakes are also an unusual, delicious way to start your day.

2515 Rogers Avenue, Fort Smith
(479) 782-8181 * Facebook.com/BensonsGrill

11

CINNAMON ROLLS
Calico County

Nearly nine million of these buttery, cinnamon-packed pastries have been ordered and consumed at this Fort Smith mainstay. The rolls, served to the table before you order, come out hot, wrapped in cloth, to enjoy while you await your meal. Locals know to pick up a dozen before they go home. These buns heat well wrapped in a slightly damp paper towel in the microwave, for a quick breakfast when they can't get over to Calico County for ham steaks, eggs made to order and chocolate gravy.

2401 South 56th Street, Fort Smith
(479) 452-3299 * calicocounty.net

HUSH PUPPIES
Catfish Hole

Slightly sweet, with a little crunchy onion inside, these perfect round balls of cornmeal and flour come to the table as part of a set-up of fixins that includes coleslaw, red onion, pickles, and green tomato relish when you order your meal. Even if you're not in the mood for catfish, fried clams, stuffed shrimp or any of the other delights the eatery offers, you can order these fixins on their own. And yes, "fixins" is the correct way to say and spell this.

24 Collum Lane West, Alma
(479) 632-9718
4127 W.est Wedington Drive, Fayetteville
(479) 521-7008
TheCatfishHole.com

13

CHICKEN FRIED STEAK
Cliff House Inn

Thousands of travelers have dived into the singular meringue-crusted Company's Comin' Pie over the years. It's the Cliff House Inn's hand-cut, hand-battered excellence of this chicken fried steak served covered in its own skillet-made gravy, tender and comforting, that should get you onto Scenic Highway Seven. Comes with an old-fashioned flour roll and two sides.

Besides, you can't beat the magnificent view of the Arkansas Grand Canyon. Open March through December.

Nine miles south and uphill
of Jasper on Scenic Highway Seven
(870) 446-2292
CliffHouseInnAR.com

CATCH YOUR OWN TROUT for DINNER
DeVito's Restaurant

You absolutely know how fresh your fish is when you catch it yourself. The trout farm, which was passed to Jim and Mary DeVito from her father, Albert Raney, Sr., has operated since the 1960s. The restaurant, opened by Jim and Mary's four sons in 1986, continues to provide marvelous Italian and American dishes.

Call in advance to fish for your own, or enjoy trout caught earlier by the family. Then you can have your catch prepared in one of eight different ways, whether it's fried trout fingers, broiled Trout Italiano with a cream sauce, broiled with pesto sauce, or even deep fried and covered with almondine sauce. Sides are included. A full slate of pasta, steak, chicken and other entrees are also offered.

350 DeVito's Loop North at Bear Creek Springs, northwest of Harrison
(870) 741-8832 * DeVitosRestaurant.com

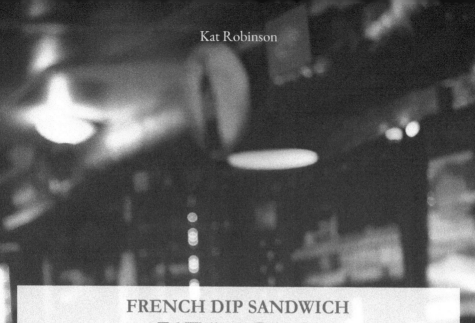

FRENCH DIP SANDWICH
Ed Walker's Drive In

While the five pound giant cheeseburger has recently earned the eatery a reputation as a foodie destination, it's this excellent roasted beef sandwich with a rich, beefy jus for dipping that first earned the Towson Avenue hotspot its place back in 1943. Great with Texas toothpicks - strings of onions and jalapenos battered, fried and served with Ranch dressing. Don't forget the pie.

1500 Towson Avenie, Fort Smith
(479) 783-3352 * EdWalkersDriveIn.org

ARKANSAS FOOD HALL of FAME
FINALIST

MAMA'S HOMEMADE MEATBALLS
Ermilio's Italian Home Cooking

There's always a line to get into this two story house along the U.S.62 B Loop through the heart of Eureka Springs. And for good reason. For decades, Ermilio's has offered remarkable housemade pastas and sauces that are offered in whatever combination you choose, whether it's gnocchi in tomato basil sauce, tri-color cheese-filled tortellini in Alfredo, or a pile of spinach fettuccini topped with Mama's Homemade Meatballs in Red Sauce, a prime Eureka Springs delicacy. Be sure to ask for and enjoy whole roasted cloves of garlic smeared onto your fresh baked bread.

26 White Street, Eureka Springs
(479) 253-8806 * Ermilios.com

17

DOUBLE DOUBLE WITH FRIES
(or the FRIED BOLOGNA SANDWICH)
Feltner's Whatta-Burger

Generations of Arkansas Tech University students have crossed Arkansas Avenue (Scenic Highway Seven) to dine at this eclectic burger joint, originally opened by Bob Feltner in 1967. Its hand-patted, griddle fried burgers are matched by massively sized orders of fries and creamy, handmade shakes. Locals also know about the real steal - the fried bologna sandwich made from Petit Jean Meats bologna, thick sliced and griddle-fried to perfection. Not affiliated with the Texas-based Whataburger chain.

1410 North Arkansas Avenue, Russellville
(479) 968-1410 * Whatta-Burger.com

ARKANSAS FOOD HALL OF FAME
FINALIST

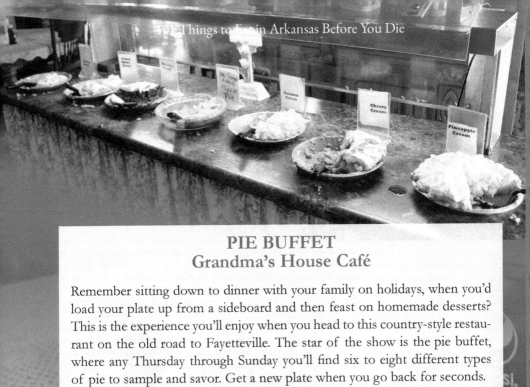

PIE BUFFET
Grandma's House Café

Remember sitting down to dinner with your family on holidays, when you'd load your plate up from a sideboard and then feast on homemade desserts? This is the experience you'll enjoy when you head to this country-style restaurant on the old road to Fayetteville. The star of the show is the pie buffet, where any Thursday through Sunday you'll find six to eight different types of pie to sample and savor. Get a new plate when you go back for seconds.

21588 U.S. Highway 71, Winslow
(479) 634-2128 * Facebook.com/GrandmasHouseCafe

19

BRIE'S COMPANY
Hammontree's Grilled Cheese

A restaurant devoted to the simple joy of cheese and bread melted together? You betcha. Corny names such as the Cheebacca, Jack to the Future and East of Edam may entertain, but this place delivers for cheese lovers of all sorts - especially with the Brie's Company with its grilled apple, caramelized onion, fig jam, and both Gouda and Brie cheeses.

326 North West Avenue #8, Fayetteville * (479) 521-1669
113 West Walnut Street, Rogers * (479) 202-5977
HammontreesCheese.com

HALF RACK OF SPARE RIBS
Herman's Ribhouse

Fayetteville's oldest restaurant celebrates porcine indulgence with delectably seasoned spare ribs and baby back ribs. You can order them by the rack, half rack or plate (three ribs with slaw or hashbrowns). Steaks, omelets, garlic chicken, housemade salsas and dressings and a famed shrimp remoulade fill out a classic menu.

2901 North College Avenue, Fayetteville
(479) 442-9671 * HermansRibhouse.com

ONE POUND BLT
Kopper Kettle Smokehouse

A pound of bacon? That's what you get when you order the BLT at Kopper Kettle Smokehouse, located between Alma and Van Buren. A pound of Petit Jean Meats bacon goes on a housemade bun. It comes to the table cut in quarters for easy sharing, if you dare. Consider also the delectable German chocolate pie when you go.

6310 Alma Highway (U.S.Highway 64), Van Buren
(479) 474-9949 * Facebook.com/KopperKettleSmokehouse

BLUE FILET PAN SEARED and PEAR PISTOU SALAD
Local Flavor Café

The constantly innovative, locally inspired menu at this Eureka Springs favorite has something for everyone, with a broad array of steaks, entrees, pastas, salads and appetizers. The Pear Pistou, with its pears and pine nuts, basil and Parmigiano Reggiano, is a refreshing memory of summer any time of the year. The prize Blue Filet Pan Seared is a perfect eight ounce handcut beef filet with an irresistible housemade Gorgonzola sauce. Don't skip the baked brie, wrapped in pastry and served with seasonal fruit.

71 South Main Street,
Eureka Springs
(479) 253-9522
LocalFlavorCafe.net

23

CHICKEN BAGLIORE
Low Gap Café

Ten miles beyond the nearest town, this former gas station along Arkansas Highway 74 doesn't look like much - but within, you'll find delectable bites from a Culinary Institutes of America trained chef. The Bottinis took over this spot and transformed it into the fanciest dive in all of Newton County. Enjoy fine steaks, seafood, and pasta dishes such as this remarkable Chicken Bagliore - chicken, broccoli and mushrooms in a creamy tomato basil sauce with penne. The cheesy biscuits are irresistible.

HC 70 Box 287, 10 miles west of Jasper
(870) 861-5848 * LowGapCafe.com

HANDMADE CHOCOLATES
Martin Greer's Candies

Dr. Martin Greer and his family create these extraordinary chocolates from century-old recipes in a variety of fashions, from lush truffles to scrumptuous barks, peanut brittle, chocolate covered apples and cherries. The two-days-to-make ambrosial chocolate-covered orange peels are ethereal. The quaint and lovely whiteclad candy shoppe near Eureka Springs is worth a detour. Chocolates and candies can be mail-ordered, but chocolates aren't shipped during the hot summer.

22151 U.S. Highway 62, Garfield (between Eureka Springs and Gateway)
(479) 656-1440 * MartinGreersCandies.com

orange peels

FAMILY STYLE CHICKEN DINNER
Monte Ne Inn Chicken

There's no menu here. Everyone receives the same family-style meal - bean soup, fresh baked bread with apple butter, fried chicken, mashed potatoes, gravy, corn, green beans, and coleslaw - as much as you want to eat. Every dish is brought to the table to share, whether you have two or twenty in your party. Dessert is extra, if you still have room.

13843 Arkansas Highway 94, Rogers
(479) 636-5511 * MonteNeInnChicken.net

PULLEYS
Neal's Café

The last place in Arkansas to offer this type of chicken portion - the center portion of the breast when it's cut into three pieces. It's served battered and pan-fried with sides. The bright pink café does Ozark country cooking, including dinners featuring this delicacy. The apple salad and cinnamon applesauce are of note, as are the high peaked pies.

806 North Thompson Street, Springdale
(479) 751-9996

FINALIST

27

NEIGHBOR'S BEST
Neighbor's Mill

The magnificent edifice built by Mike and Karin Nabors resembles an old mill. Within, the patient crafting of breads, sweets and other eats makes it a must-visit destination. Loaves rise and head to the oven six days a week in so many varieties, including white and olive, cranberry orange and blueberry cream, even asiago cracked black pepper. Neighbor's Best, in particular, is a marvelous nine-grain bread, perfect for any sandwich.

1012 U.S. Highway 65 North, Harrison * (870) 741-6455
2090 West Pleasant Grove Road, Rogers * (479) 282-3488
NeiighborsMill.com

BREAKFAST WITH CATHEAD BISCUITS
Oark General Store

Oversized, pliant, tasty - the cathead biscuits are wonders all their own, called such because they're literally big as the head of the average domesticated feline. The drive to the oldest general store in Arkansas is fabulous, whether its along the Mulberry River on Arkansas Highway 215 or coming up Arkansas Highway 103 from Clarksville. No cell signal, but there is free wi-fi.

10360 County Road 5440, Oark
(479) 292-3351 * OarkGeneralStore.com

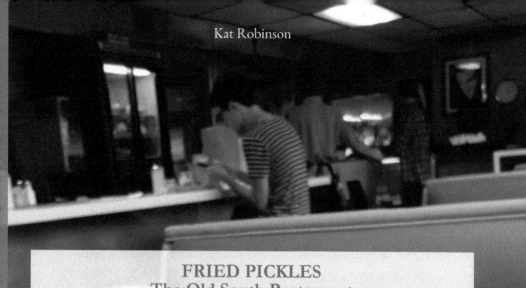

FRIED PICKLES
The Old South Restaurant

There are a lot of reasons to recommend The Old South - Friday prime rib nights, Kansas City steaks, fried chicken, salads with the restaurant's famed salad dressing, diner-style breakfasts, possum pie - but for a singular dish, it'd have to be the Bernell Austin-style fried pickle planks, similar (but not identical) to the original fried pickles created in nearby Atkins. Comes with Ranch dressing, but if you ask they'll throw in some Old South salad dressing for dipping, too.

1330 East Main Street, Russellville
(479) 968-3789 * OldSouthRestaurant.net

THE EXCALIBURGER
Ozark Café

Often imitated, this is the original thick, oversized cheeseburger sandwiched between two grilled cheese sandwiches. It's famous, but just one of so many features on a packed menu that includes chocolate gravy and buttermilk biscuits, eight inch wide pancakes and the Volcano Burger - which comes with a halo of fried cheese.

107 East Court Street, Jasper
(870) 446-2976 * OzarkCafe.com

VEAL SALTIMBOCCO FLORENTINE
and the ITALIAN PLATTER
Taliano's Italian Restaurant

Opened in 1970 in the 1887 Sparks Mansion by the Caldarera family, this gorgeous restaurant offers classic Italian dishes and pasta in an elegant, perfectly restored and preserved Renaissance Revival home. Since then, generations have come to Taliano's to celebrate romance, marriages, anniversaries, birthdays and a love for the good Italian food served here. The Veal Saltimbocco Florentine with its ham and spinach layers between cheese and perfectly sauteed veal is a marvelous delight. Indecisive diners should head straight for the Italian Platter, which offers cannelloni, chicken cacciatore, ravioli and meatballs all on the same platter. The soft Italian bread, delectably cheesy baked artichokes, delightful creamy tortoni and a cup of cappuccino with a slice of tiramisu are all equally stupendous.

201 North 14th Street, Fort Smith
(479) 785-2292 * Talianos.net

BMF CHICKEN
The Hive

The esteemed Chef Matthew McClure, a six times James Beard Best Chef: South semifinalist and *Food and Wine*'s 2015 selection for The People's Best New Chef Midwest, continues to serve Arkansas cuisine on an elevated level, whether it's his Berkshire Hog Chop with creamed corn, homemade buttermilk ice cream, or even the simple pimento cheese and bacon jam sandwich. But it's this dish, named by *Men's Journal* as the best fried chicken in the entire United States, that shows the expertise of McClure and his incredible team. Crisp, tender, perfect, especially with that to-die-for seasoned honey. Sundays or by arranged appointment only.

200 Northeast A Street, Bentonville (inside the 21c Museum Hotel)
(479) 286-6575 * TheHiveBentonville.com

33

CHARCUTERIE PLATE
Tusk and Trotter

This friendly gastropub created from Sam Walton's original Bentonville office is a laidback, unapologetically hearty place to grab a beer and an exceptional entree crafted from locally raised beef, pork, poultry and other livestock. Chef Rob Nelson's dedication to building relationships with farms and producers is evident. His exploration of Arkansas heritage roots in smoking techniques, sausages and condiments shows in unusual but familiar dishes. For instance, there's the Catfish Pastami Reuben, where pastrami is made from catfish in-house. See The Hogzilla with ground boar, housemade bacon and jowl jam. And check out the braised lamb shank called Bone With A Hole. Tusk and Trotter's charcuterie board showcases the heart of what the eatery has to offer - handmade meatballs, country pâté, smoked salmon, local artisanal cheeses, pickled vegetables, pepper jelly, capers, fresh ground mustard and the only true legislated Arkansas bacon (made from pork butt instead of belly) currently offered on a restaurant menu in the state. Nominated twice for Best Restaurant in the South by *Southern Living*.

110 Southeast A Street, Bentonville
(479) 268-4494 * TuskAndTrotter.com

FRIED CHICKEN AND SPAGHETTI
The Venesian Inn

Originally opened in 1947, this family-run restaurant in Tontitown continues to serve the regional specialty of fried chicken and spaghetti, rolls and Italian soaked salad to diners in a classic homestyle restaurant setting.

Each dinner comes with a soaked salad of lettuce in a garlic vinaigrette and a basket of hot rolls accompanied by pats of butter. Pouring honey onto your rolls is expected.

582 West Henri De Tonti Boulevard, Tontitown
(479) 361-2562 * TheVenesianInn.com

ARKANSAS FOOD HALL of FAME
WINNER

35

CHEESE FONDUE
Wiederkehr Weinkeller

Situated within a wine cellar dug in 1880 by Johannes Wiederkehr himself, this Swiss restaurant is a prime place to indulge after a day of wine tours in the Altus Viticultural Region. The restaurant and winery offers Swiss favorites such as Quiche Lorraine and Poulet Roti au Vin Blanc. It's the fondue, this incomparable blend of cheeses, spices and wine served in a hot pot, that will quite literally warm your heart. Best shared. Be sure to peruse the wine list, which includes not only Wiederkehr wines but varietals from both within Arkansas and domestic and international treasures as well.

3324 Swiss Family Drive, Wiederkehr Village
(479) 468-9463 * WiederkehrWines.com

MEATLOAF
The Wooden Spoon

With a menu that includes such family favorites as fried catfish, substantial sandwiches, and a vast array of heritage and family recipe pies, it may seem odd to single out the humble meatloaf as the best thing you should try at this restaurant. But you'll find no better verion of the comfort food favorite than what comes to the table within an old horse barn along Arkansas Highway 59. Expect a line, nd be sure to make room for pie.

1000 South Gentry Boulevard, Gentry
(479) 736-3030 * WoodenSpoonGentry.com

37

NORTH CENTRAL

- [ ] Bulldog Restaurant, Bald Knob
- [ ] Carol's Lakeview Restaurant, Cherokee Village
- [ ] Coursey's Smoked Meats, St. Joe
- [ ] Daisy's Lunchbox, Searcy
- [ ] Gaston's First Class Restaurant, Lakeview
- [ ] Holy Smokes BBQ, Mountain Home
- [ ] Kenda Drive In, Marshall
- [ ] PJ's Rainbow Café, Mountain View
- [ ] Red Apple Inn, Heber Springs
- [ ] Shorty's Restaurant, Providence
- [ ] Tommy's Famous A Pizzeria, Mountain View

STRAWBERRY SHORTCAKE
Bulldog Restaurant

From April through early summer each year, folks head to Bald Knob for the satisfaction of this heralded dessert made only when Arkansas strawberries are available. Crisp, cookie-like shortbread is topped with fresh, sweet and tart slices of strawberries, whipped cream and pecans. A coveted treasure served for a short time. If you happen to miss strawberry season, the Bulldog offers a peach shortcake made from fresh local peaches in mid to late summer.

3614 Arkansas Highway 367, Bald Knob
(501) 724-5195

BREAKFAST and BLUEBERRY RHUBARB PIE
Carol's Lakeview Restaurant

The heart of Cherokee Village offers tasty food for really low prices across the street from Lake Thunderbird. Pancakes come big as a plate; the hashbrown skillet plate is an extraordinarily filling meatless meal. The pies are extraordinary, with the tallest cream pies in the state offered here in pineapple and peanut versions. But it's the blueberry rhubarb, made from rhubarb the family grows and not at all bitter, that is the true standout here.

200 Iroquois Drive,
Cherokee Village
(870) 257-3595

SMOKED HAM
Coursey's Smoked Meats

Lynn Coursey, a New York chef, moved to Arkansas and started this smoke-house back in 1945. Today the third, fourth and fifth generations of his family often appear behind the counter at this must-stop destination along U.S. Highway 65. Coursey's takes Petit Jean Meats' hams, smokes them for hours, and offers them by the pound, sliced how you like. You can also purchase a whole ham, or a smoked turkey breast, smoked bacon, smoked sausages and even cheeses and beef jerky. Travelers know to look for snack bags of smoked turkey and smoked cheese by the register; if they're out, ask for a quarter pound chopped - it comes out to the same price.

152 Courseys Road, just off U.S. Highway 65 at St Joe
(870) 439-2503

CHICKEN SALAD and CINNAMON ROLLS
Daisy's Lunchbox

This adorable café is home to the most cinnamon-y cinnamon rolls you can find anywhere in Arkansas, buttery rounds that come at the end of every meal. The honey pecan chicken salad is also irresistable, both decadent and reminiscent of summer picnics. Allot time for a leisurely lunch.

311 North Spruce Street on the courthouse square, Searcy
(501) 281-0297

PAN-FRIED TROUT WITH NEPTUNE SAUCE
Gaston's First Class Restaurant

This white-tablecloth dining experience over the White River is the perfect location to end a day of trout fishing, relaxing or observing the resort's white peacocks. Chef Rick will cook your catch or trout from the kitchen in this delicate preparation, topped with a shrimp and lump crabmeat Béarnaise and served elegantly with river views.

1777 River Road, Lakeview
(870) 431-5202 * Gastons.com

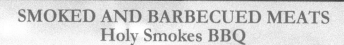

SMOKED AND BARBECUED MEATS
Holy Smokes BBQ

Decadently smoked ribs, chicken breasts, pastrami, turkey, hams and briskets all shine on the menu at this jovial hotspot on Mountain Home's northeast side. These excellent dishes are available here and at the restaurant's food truck, which can be found at all sorts of local gatherings, festivals and wherever fun is happening in North Central Arkansas.

400 Arkansas Highway 201, Mountain Home
(870) 425-8080

CHOCOLATE ROLL
Kenda Drive-In

The oldest and only continually operating drive-in theater in the state opened in 1966 in Marshall. Every night, The Kenda Drive-In shows a first-run movie on its singular screen - two on weekend nights. The concession stand serves far more than popcorn. Its smashy burgers and generous orders of popcorn topped with real melted butter are excellent.

Searcy County, where the Kenda is located, is the home of a special dessert, the chocolate roll. This pastry is filled with cocoa powder, powdered sugar and butter and makes for a great hand-held treat. Look for them in a tin on the end of the counter, near the cash register. Cash only.

107 Westwood Drive, Marshall
(870) 448-5400 * KendaDriveIn.com

THE OMWICH
PJ's Rainbow Café

A classic small town country dinette half a block off the courthouse square, there's something to see in every direction - including on the ceiling. PJ's Rainbow Café, a longstanding mainstay in the community, has become the go-to place for families looking for a good home-cooked meal away from home, by locals who enjoy breakfast and lunch with friends, and by pie lovers eager to try whatever's on the whiteboard each day. The extensive breakfast menu includes an extraordinary variety of egg-and-meat combinations, with selections including fried bologna, pork tenderloin, liver and onion, Polish sausage and corned beef hash in addition to ham, bacon and sausage. The Omwich improves even more, combining a two egg omelet filled with a choice of ingredients and cheese - easy to eat, the perfect handheld to tackle before spending a day in the Folk Music Capital of the World.

216 West Main Street, Mountain View
(870) 269-8633 * Facebook.com
/PJsRainbowCafe

THAI STYLE HALIBUT
Red Apple Inn

For generations, this expansive, elegant restaurant overlooking Greers Ferry Lake has offered celebrated steaks, decadent breakfasts and its famed desserts in a gorgeous setting. Its Thai Style Halibut, a unique presentation of fresh halibut seared and drizzled with a Thai-style coconut sauce over quinoa and vegetables, is a masterpiece befitting such a setting.

305 Club Road, Heber Springs
(501) 362-3111 * RedAppleInn.com

BEANS AND CORNBREAD
Shorty's Restaurant

Simple, hearty, satisfying, this old fashioned dairy diner in the Providence community makes one of the best versions of the old Arkansas favorite you'll find in a restaurant. It's just one treasure in an eatery that celebrates country delights such as homemade jams and jellies, coleslaw, fried bologna sandwiches, fried catfish with all the fixings, and beautifully constructed meringue pies. A real hidden delight.

3393 Arkansas Highway 157, Judsonia
(501) 729-4777

ANY PIZZA
Tommy's Famous A Pizzeria

Detroit-style crust. Chicago-style crust. Clean air and clean water and the atmosphere of Mountain View. It all comes together at the Miller family pizza joint on the town's west side, where since 1990 Tommy's has offered pizza and barbecue from a converted house with peach-painted walls, from old fashioned gas powered ovens. The crisp-edge crust and tangy sauce work with all sorts of pies here, from combinations like the Fat Boy to unusual ingredients such as walnuts and zucchini, and unless you ask for something different, it comes out sliced in squares.

West Main (Arkansas Highway 66) and Famous Place, Mountain View
(870) 269-3278 * tommysfamous.net

49

UPPER DELTA

- [ ] Batten's Bakery, Paragould
- [ ] Dixie Pig, Blytheville
- [ ] Dondie's White River Princess, Des Arc
- [ ] Howard's Donuts, West Memphis
- [ ] Lackey's Smoke House BBQ, Newport
- [ ] Lazzari Italian Oven, Jonesboro
- [ ] Parkview Restaurant, Corning
- [ ] Tacker's Shake Shack, Marion
- [ ] Tamale Factory, Gregory
- [ ] Wilson Café, Wilson

OLD FASHIONED CHOCOLATE FRIED PIES
Batten's Bakery

Just like grandma used to make, these fried pies are rolled dough folded in half over a blend of butter, cocoa powder and powdered sugar, deep fried and doughnut glazed for the perfect handheld treat. While other chocolate fried pies have a custard filling, Batten's version comes out firm. When hot, it rivals the flavor of a chocolate chip cookie. Cold milk and hot coffee are on hand for best enjoyment.

1735 Paragould Plaza, Paragould
(870) 236-7810 * BattensBakery.com

51

PIG SANDWICH
Dixie Pig

The Halsell Family's esteemed eatery, dating back to the days of the Rustic Inn in 1923, still serves its most favored and distinguished entry into Arkansas's culinary landscape, a mound of smoked pork with coleslaw on a seedless bun. This pig sandwich has brought generations to the table to consume and enjoy pork from the smoker with the restaurant's hard to beat vinegar-style sauce.

701 North 6th Street, Blytheville

(870) 763-4636

ARKANSAS
FOOD
HALL of FAME

FINALIST

SEAFOOD BUFFET
Dondie's White River Princess

There are few finer views in the Upper Delta than those offered from the decks and stories of Dondie's, a purpose-built restaurant resembling a steamboat along the White River in Des Arc. Within, you'll find hot catfish, fried chicken strips, clam strips, boiled and fried shrimp and (in season) boiled crawfish to consume to your heart's content. Menu service and an outrageous variety of desserts available; reservations recommended.

203 East Curran Street, Des Arc
(870) 256-3311

53

GERMAN CHOCOLATE CAKE DOUGHNUTS
Howard's Do-Nuts

You've never enjoyed German chocolate cake like this. The crispy edges of this doughnut, its light pastry, and a toasted-coconut custard top make this one of the most incredible doughnuts conjured in Arkansas. Howard's also offers Arkansas Delta-style doughnuts, where the fillings are on top rather inside each round.

1711 North Missouri Street, West Memphis
(870) 735-2046

LACKEY'S TAMALES
Lackey's Smoke House BBQ

These Cajun-spiced, chicken filled tamales wrapped in corn husks might float below your radar. But Clint Lackey's original recipe still stands out as one of the singularly delectable tamales you'll find in the Arkansas Delta. Many choose to consume the filling of these corn husks with crackers. They're an excellent match with a plate of barbecue, hush puppies with dressing (a restaurant favorite), or covered in cheese dip. Get some frozen to take home with you for later.

601 Malcolm Avenue, Newport
(870) 217-0228 * Facebook.com/LackeysSmokeHouse

55

CRABMEAT CANNELLONI
Lazzari Italian Oven

A longstanding favorite of Arkansas State University students on a budget, this family-friendly Italian joint serves up classics with an authentic flair. From the signature Mista salad to the hearty sesame seed-encrusted bread served with both butter and olive oil, every meal is a winner. The crabmeat cannelloni, with a filling of lump crabmeat, scallops and shrimp, comes smothered in an asiago-parmesan cream sauce with mushrooms, a decadent dish that would be twice the price anywhere else.

2230 South Caraway Road, Jonesboro
(870) 931-4700 * LazzariItalianOven.com

CHICKEN SPECIAL
Parkview Restaurant

Not for those in a hurry. This is a whole chicken the cook dresses, batters, fries and serves with four potato halves, fresh from the fryer. The hot, juicy fried chicken is a steal, and an excellent dinner for two. The daily boards show what sides are available, and usually feature the likes of brown beans, corn, turnip greens, raspberry fluff, hominy, cantaloupe or glazed carrots. Get the coconut cream pie before you head out the door.

1617 West Main Street, Corning
(870) 857-3513

57

THE SULTANA CHALLENGE BURGER
Tacker's Shake Shack

Many have tried but few have conquered the immense, towering creation that's the crazy star at this family-run operation. The burger is named for the worst maritime disaster in U.S. history, the explosion of the riverboat *Sultana* with 2,137 aboard on April 27th, 1865. This burger's four beef patties, bacon, egg, cheese, hashbrowns and chili is enough to sink a ship. Those who eat it in 30 minutes or less receive a T-shirt and their photo on the wall. A host of other creative burgers, plus catfish, daily plate lunch specials and a dizzying array of pies also shine.

409 East Military Road, Marion
(870) 739-3943 * ShakeMarion.com

HALF A DOZEN TAMALES WITH CHILI and a STEAK
Tamale Factory

George Eldridge, the man who brought Doe's Eat Place to Little Rock, takes great pride in the tamales served at his establishment. Needing a place to make those tamales, he came up with an idea and purposed half a horse barn he was building at his farm in Gregory to a kitchen where those famous Doe's tamales could be made. Later, he opened up that barn on Friday and Saturday nights to serve not only those tamales but those excellent Porterhouse and T-Bone steaks for which Doe's became famous. Somehow, the drive to this distant barn in the Upper Delta makes this extra tasty.

19751 Highway 33 South, Gregory
(870) 347-1350 * TheTamaleFactory.net

59

SMOKED CHICKEN LEG SANDWICH
Wilson Café

Joe Cartwright and Shari' Haley opened the old tavern on the Wilson square at the end of December 2013, one of the first steps in the revitalization of the former company town. The two have crafted an Arkansas New Delta menu utilizing modern techniques and produce raised right across the street at Wilson Gardens to cultivate a fresh, innovative and ever-changing menu. Be sure to share a slice of the restaurant's remarkable doughnut bread pudding with someone you love.

2 North Jefferson Street, on the square in Wilson
(870) 655-0222 * EatAtWilson.com

LOWER DELTA

- [ ] Colonial Steak House, Pine Bluff
- [ ] Country Village Oven Bakery, Star City
- [ ] Craig Brothers Bar-B-Q Café, De Valls Bluff
- [ ] Hoots BBQ, McGehee
- [ ] Jones Bar-B-Q Diner, Marianna
- [ ] Kibb's BBQ #2, Stuttgart/Pine Bluff
- [ ] Molly's Diner, Warren
- [ ] Murry's Restaurant, Hazen
- [ ] Pasquale's Tamales, Helena-West Helena
- [ ] Pickens Restaurant and Store, Pickens
- [ ] Rhoda's Famous Hot Tamales and Pies, Lake Village
- [ ] Taylor's Steakhouse, Dumas

ROAST PRIME RIB OF BEEF
Colonial Steak House

For 45 years, this Tudor-style 1912 elementary school building has been Pine Bluff's place to go for anniversaries, wedding rehearsals and important dates. Colonial Steak House prides itself on its generous, hand-cut steaks, and its most impressive is the Roast Prime Rib of Beef, a two pound collossus served with its own jus, preferably to a couple. The ample offering is tender and succulent, accompanied by garlic bread and a side of your choice. It always makes an impression. The savory French onion soup, crispy Cotton Blossoms and luscious Black Bottom pie are all worthy choices to round out your visit.

111 West 8th Avenue, Pine Bluff
(870) 536-3488 * TheColonialSteakHouse.com

FRESH BAKED ROLLS with HONEY BUTTER
Country Village Oven Bakery

Nestled into a crafters' village between a boot store and a taxidermy shop, this bakery produces country-style breads, cakes, cinnamon rolls, pies, jams, relishes and doughnuts, all delightfully handcrafted. The best, simple pleasure to be found here is tender, pliant hand rolls, which are best served with butter blended in the shop with honey from a local apiary. A real blessing.

220 Knight Haven Circle, Star City
(870) 628-3683

63

PORK SANDWICH HOT
Craig Brothers Bar-B-Q Café

Lawrence and Wes Craig started this shop along US Highway 70 way back in 1947. The family still runs the eatery under the eye of Lawrence's son Robert and longtime family friends, Jerry and Joyce Surratt.

The joint's location at De Valls Bluff, close to the halfway point between Little Rock and Memphis, makes it an ideal stop. Folks swear by the smoky barbecue pork and beef and by the three different levels of heat offered with the unique, spice-packed sauce. True afficianados know to get theirs hot, and order a Pepsi to cut the heat. Messy delicious.

15 Walnut Street (US Highway 70), De Valls Bluff
(870) 998-2616

BRISKET STUFFED BAKED POTATO
Hoots BBQ

Honestly, anything with brisket here is good, as Hoots manages to deliver with the best brisket in the state. The smoked chicken is also fall-apart fantastic, and the smoked pork is juicy. Add an order of the excellent hand-battered onion rings for maximum enticement.

2008 U.S. Highway 65, McGehee
(870) 222-1234

65

PORK SANDWICH wi' SLAW
Jones Bar-B-Q Diner

Arkansas's only James Beard Foundation America's Classics award winner has a rather short menu - sandwiches of smoked pork with or without coleslaw, or smoked pork by the pound. That's it, unless you want a can of Coke or a bag of chips to take with you. Still, the pork smoked and the sauce blended the same way since the Civil War is worth a drive from wherever you are. Come early - when Mr. Harold Jones runs out of meat, that's it for the day.

219 West Louisiana Street, Marianna
(870) 295-3807 * Facebook.com/JonesBarBQDiner

ARKANSAS FOOD HALL·FAME
WINNER

RIB TIPS
Kibb's BBQ #2

Sloppy, soaked pork rib tips served by the dinner or pound makes for a savory, piquant meal. Kibb's BBQ is a family affair, with locations in Stuttgart and Pine Bluff (the Kibbs grandchildren have their own North Little Rock location called Grand Kibb's). The sauce has a bite, the smoke is hickory, and the menu is packed with meats. Another choice to consider: the smoked beef sandwich dressed with mayonnaise, lettuse and tomato instead of sauce. Grab the napkins.

1102 East Harrison Street, Stuttgart * (870) 673-2072
1400 South Blake Street, Pine Bluff * (870) 535-8400
2117 University Drive, Pine Bluff *(870) 535-6563

67

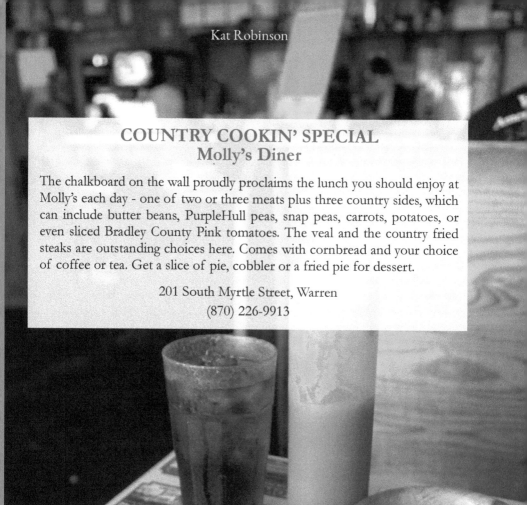

COUNTRY COOKIN' SPECIAL
Molly's Diner

The chalkboard on the wall proudly proclaims the lunch you should enjoy at Molly's each day - one of two or three meats plus three country sides, which can include butter beans, PurpleHull peas, snap peas, carrots, potatoes, or even sliced Bradley County Pink tomatoes. The veal and the country fried steaks are outstanding choices here. Comes with cornbread and your choice of coffee or tea. Get a slice of pie, cobbler or a fried pie for dessert.

201 South Myrtle Street, Warren
(870) 226-9913

SEAFOOD PLATTER
Murry's Restaurant

Ogden Murry's reputation for having some of the best catfish in the South is carried on by his son-in-law Stanley Young and Young's wife Becky. When you enter the doors, you have made friends, and you're sitting down with family. Buttered bread comes to the table hot while you're dithering over the menu, which features duck and steak and quail. If you choose this seafood platter, you'll get a sampling, with a stuffed crab and substantially large shrimp, a baked potato, cylindrical hush puppies, cole slaw and light, heaven's gift perfect fillets of catfish .Save room for the buttery rum sauce-clad bread pudding... and a nap afterwards.

U.S. Highway 70 East, between Carlisle and Hazen
(870) 255-3266

TAMALE PLATE
Pasquale's Tamales

A family recipe that goes back to a Sicilian immigrant who came to the United States in the 1890s, Pasquale's premium choice-cut beef filled tamales are an extraordinary joy. Add in Joe St. Columbia's perfect beanless chili, a handfull of Cheddar, chopped white onions and jalapeno slices, and you have an irresistible dish of Arkansas Delta divinity. Saltines make a great scoop. Fridays and Saturdays only.

1005 Little Rock Road (U.S. Highway 49), Helena-West Helena
(870) 338-3991 * SuckTheShuck.com

ARKANSAS FOOD HALL OF FAME

FINALIST
2022-23

BAKED CHICKEN and SQUASH DRESSING
Pickens Store and Restaurant

Named for Reuben Augustus Pickens, who settled with his family in the area in 1881, this oversized Quonset style building houses a post office, shop and this eatery, known for its home cookin'. Lunch comes with three sides - you choose them and whether you want a meat or not. The slightly sweet squash dressing could be enjoyed on its own. It usually comes alongside other Delta-style sides like brown gravy-doused rice and fried cabbage. The baked chicken is melt-off-the-bone tender. Be sure to save room for a slice of pie.

122 Pickens Road, Pickens
(870) 382-5266

HOT TAMALES
Rhoda's Famous Hot Tamales and Pies

Rhoda Adams and her family continue to operate one of the most legendary soul food cafés you'll find in the state. The tamales, filled with a mixture of chicken fat and beef, are hand-rolled once a week and boiled as needed. Travelers come get a mess to take back with them to all corners of the region. For those ordering two dozen or more, the tamales are carefully packed in new, clean coffee cans. They freeze beautifully.

Rhoda's sweet potato, pecan and half-and-half pies are so good, they eventually were added to the sign. If you're too stuffed from the tamales and can't eat a whole pie, mini pies are almost always ready for you. Her fried chicken is also on-par with the best in the state, and burgers and daily specials are also spot-on. You can't go wrong here.

714 Saint Mary's Street, Lake Village
(870) 265-3108

ARKANSAS
FOOD
HALL of FAME
WINNER

PORTERHOUSE FOR TWO
Taylor's Steakhouse

This out-of-town steakhouse started life as Taylor's Grocery all the way back in 1954. Charles and Dorothy's dry goods and sundry store evolved over time, first to a convenient grocery and lunch counter. Dorothy's penchant for barbecue lead to son Chuck's interest in culinary fare, and as the years passed grocery shelves were taken out in favor of tables for hungry eaters. Today, Chuck and his wife Pam manage the restaurant and cook for crowds. The extraordinary 28 day aged steaks have earned a fantastic reputation for quality and flavor. If you make it through one of the big slabs, try the white chocolate bread pudding. You might want a driver to get you home.

14201 Arkansas Highway 54, Dumas
(870) 382-5349

SOUTHWEST

- ☐ 4-Dice Restaurant, Fordyce
- ☐ Burl's Country Smokehouse, Royal
- ☐ Burge's Smoked Turkeys and Hams, Lewisville/Little Rock
- ☐ Cattleman's Steak House, Texarkana
- ☐ The Dairyette, Mt. Ida
- ☐ Dannie's Café, Hope
- ☐ DeLuca's Pizzeria Napoletana, Hot Springs
- ☐ Herb's Creamland, Ashdown
- ☐ Keeney's Food Market, Malvern
- ☐ McClard's Bar-B-Q, Hot Springs
- ☐ Minute Man Restaurant, El Dorado
- ☐ The Ohio Club, Hot Springs
- ☐ The Pancake Shop, Hot Springs
- ☐ Ray's Hamburgers, Monticello
- ☐ Rolando's Nuevo Latino Restaurante, Hot Springs/Fort Smith/Fayetteville
- ☐ The Shack, Jessieville
- ☐ Skyline Café, Mena
- ☐ The Smokin' Bull, Emerson
- ☐ The Spudnut Shoppe, El Dorado
- ☐ Stubby's Hik'ry Pit Bar-B-Q, Hot Springs
- ☐ Woods Place, Camden

SEAFOOD BUFFET
4-Dice Restaurant

This spot opened along the bypass in 1967. Its claim to fame could be its Friday and Saturday night seafood buffet, with peel-and-eat shrimp, fried catfish, broiled catfish, clam strips, fried shrimp, stuffed crabs and all the sides plus enormous cinnamon rolls for dessert. But it's the tenuous connection with the Rolling Stones, per a visit by Ron Wood and Keith Richards on July 5th, 1975 on their way to Dallas, and their subsequent arrest a few miles down the road, that set this eatery into its very own place in rock and roll history. Sunday buffet adds fried chicken and salisbury steak in gravy.

1990 U.S. Highway 167, Fordyce
(870) 352-5815

ARKANSAS
FOOD
HALL of FAME

FINALIST

SMOKED MEATS AND CHEESES
Burl's Country Smokehouse

Much ado has been made of this longtime roadside attraction's cinnamon rolls, which are as of this writing the largest sold within the state of Arkansas. But the smokehouse's fine pork links, Genoa salami, turkey, beef brisket, ham, corned beef, roast beef, Canadian bacon and pastrami, alongside a collection of cheeses, makes this the place to pick up sandwiches to take along on any Lake Ouachita fishing trip. The smoked but not peppered jerky is also a favorite.

10176 Albert Pike Road, Royal
(501) 991-3875

TURKEY SALAD SANDWICH
Burge's Smoked Turkeys and Hams

Alden Burge's backyard smoker is where this tradition began back in the 1950s. Folks who enjoyed his smoked turkey and hams before football games encouraged him to buy a Dairyette in town, and thus Burge's was born. A second location opened in 1977 in Little Rock. Every week of Thanksgiving and Christmas, there's a constant line at the Little Rock shop as the capitol city gets its holiday turkey. This particular turkey salad, made from the house smoked turkey, is so irresistible, locals call it "turkey crack." Enjoy it in a sandwich or on the restaurant's famed "leftover plate" in a scoop alongside tomato, peach slices, cottage cheese and crackers.

526 Spruce Street, Lewisville * (800) 921-4292
5620 R Street, Little Rock * (501) 666-1660
SmokedTurkeys.com

ARKANSAS
FOOD
HALL of FAME
WINNER

77

KING CUT PRIME RIB and CALF FRIES
Cattleman's Steak House

Roy Oliver opened this high-class, wood-panelled establishment in 1964 across State Line Avenue from Texas. Today it remains the city's prime prom night and anniversary celebration location, with extraordinarily tender steaks, savory quail, and cast iron broiled and blackened red snapper. The exemplary prime rib is butter-soft, with an excellent jus and horseradish. Cattleman's runs a special on prime rib on Tuesday night, which makes sharing that King Cut even more attractive.

For the more adventuresome, the restaurant offers a variety of "fries," in particular calf fries and turkey fries, battered and fried portions of testicles served with marinara sauce. The less exotic but spicier dragon fries are actualy stuffed, battered and fried jalapenos.

4018 North State Line Avenue, Texarkana
(870) 774-4481 * CattlemansSteakHouseTexarkana.com

CHOCOLATE MALT
The Dairyette

Summer around Lake Ouachita requires a visit to this old fashioned dairy diner with both a dining room and walk-up windows. The extensive menu covers every hit, from burgers to chili dogs to chicken salad sandwiches, wraps, catfish and hamburger steak dinners and a full board of drinks and ice cream delights. In the decades since it opened in 1958, generations have come to pick up a sack of burgers with crinkle cut fries, milkshakes and banana splits, and even the generously thick chocolate malts. Expect a wait on the weekends.

717 U.S. Highway 270, Mount Ida
(870) 867-2312 * Facebook.com/Dairyette

HALF RACK OF NEW ZEALAND LAMB
Dannie's Café

This barn some distance outside Hope looks like it should be a country diner. Instead, it serves Harissa Lamb Tacos, Bofungo and pots of chocolate. The delectable New Zealand lamb is spiced and roasted expertly for this gorgeous dish. Owing to the remote location, dishes do run out, so make reservations.

475 County Road 54, Hope
(870) 777-8870 * Facebook.com/DanniesCafe

FRANKY'S FLATBUSH
DeLuca's Pizzeria Napoletana

The sauce: kosher salt and tomatoes from Naples. The simple dough. Rounds of fresh Mozzarella. A 725-degree oven. These simple ingredients are rendered extraordinary in the hands of Anthony Valinoti, the former businessman turned pizza troubadour, whose charismatic energy elevates every dough-borne creation to a communal experience amongst friends. Call ahead to reserve your dough, especially on the weekends.

831 Central Avenue, Hot Springs National Park
(501) 609-9002 * Facebook.com/DelucasPizzeriaNapoletana

THE RANDY DANDY
Herb's Creamland

Herb Candless opened his eponymous dairy diner in 1954, and continued to run it until his untimely death in 2013. Today the family still sells plate lunches, burgers and deli sandwiches at this community favorite. Of note is the Randy Dandy, a hoagie roll filled with smoked ham and turkey, Swiss and mozzarella cheeses, and your choice of dressing.

116 Dutch Webster Drive, Ashdown
(870) 898-2200

RIBEYE STEAK LUNCH
Keeney's Food Market

Charles Keeney opened his grocery in Malvern back in 1956. He and his wife Maureen kept it going long after larger retailers moved into the area. Around 2000, they started serving breakfast and lunch to customers in the deli at the back of the store. Today, Keeney's is one of the state's most charming hidden gems, with ribs, pork chops, burgers and steaks listed alongside sandwiches and sides on a menu dotted with grocery price stickers. On Thursdays, Mr. Keeney pulls out the ribeyes, twelve ounce flamekist wonders served on paper plates, informal but oh so satisfying.

101 West Mill Street, Malvern
(501) 332-3371
Facebook.com/KeeneysFoodMarket

ARKANSAS FOOD HALL OF FAME
WINNER

83

RIBS AND FRY and a WHOLE TAMALE SPREAD
McClard's Bar-B-Q

Since 1928, the McClard family has served smoked meats, tamales, and its signature sauce up to visitors from close by and far off. The classic whitewashed building along Albert Pike is almost always packed with hungry diners who have followed its most famous patron, President Bill Clinton, to see what the buzz is all about. Locals know if they want a hearty meal, to dive into the venerable ribs and fry plate - a mess of ribs topped with a pile of hot fries. Tamales are always in favor here, and the tremendous Whole Spread covers two of those fat tamales with baked beans, shredded smoked beef, onions, cheese and Fritos for an overload of flavor.

505 Albert Pike Road, Hot Springs
(501) 623-9665 * McClards.com

ARKANSAS
FOOD
HALL of FAME

WINNER

A NO. 2 or a NO. 6
Minute Man Restaurant

This last vestige of the original Wes Hall operation that once spanned several states with hundreds of locations can still be relied upon to give you the flavor of those original burgers, whether it's Hall's hickory smoke sauce on the Number 2 or the relish sauce, lettuce and tomato on a Salad Burger. New locations are expected to be opened in Little Rock in 2020.

318 West Main Street,
El Dorado
(870) 862-7995
MinuteManBurgers.com

minute man.

*remember when you're hungry...
it only takes a minute man!*

85

THE BUGSY
The Ohio Club

The Spa City has a connection with corned beef, from the earliest days of operation for Oaklawn Racing Park and its Eisenberg corned beef sandwiches. The Ohio Club elevates that common sliced meat with The Bugsy, the superb combination of corned beef with pastrami, Swiss cheese and stone-ground mustard on rye. Pair it with the excellent whole fried okra for a good club-eats bite at Arkansas's oldest bar, originally opened in 1905.

336 Central Avenue,
Hot Springs National Park
(501) 627-0702 * TheOhioClub.com

ARKANSAS
FOOD
HALL of FAME

FINALIST

APPLE PANCAKES
The Pancake Shop

Expect a wait when you come to enjoy the classic diner experience at The Pancake Shop, which has operated near Bathhouse Row since 1940. It's worth the extra time (which you can spend next door perusing The Savory Pantry's wares) to take one of the green-clad seats and enjoy oversized pancakes, house-spiced sausage, gigantic ham steaks, omelets, site-made apple butter and grape jelly, and the hottest coffee in town. Pancakes come in traditional and buckwheat varieties with or without banana, blueberries, or apples - the latter of which has an extraordinary flavor reminiscent of a holiday morning.

216 Central Avenue, Hot Springs National Park
(501) 624-5720 * PancakeShop.com

DOUBLE BACON CHEESEBURGER
Ray's Hamburgers

Handpatted, old fashioned beef burgers, barbecue, dinners and sandwiches pack the menu at Monticello's local hangout, which also delivers well on ice cream confections and fried pies. Juicy hamburger patties on griddle-crisped buns with an ample addition of bacon and cheese is one sure way to get your motor running.

207 U.S. Highway 425, Monticello
(870) 367-3292

PLATO DE AVENTURA
Rolando's Nuevo Latino Restaurante

Rolando and Sherri Cuzco's art-meets-Latin American aesthetic is at the heart of this collection of gorgeously lush restaurants with an equally lavish menu that elevates simple fare to colorful, exuberant celebrations. The star of the menu, whether it's the lunch portion (pictured) or the evening option, is the Plato de Aventura - a chicken or pork quesadilla, chicken enchilada, taquito or tamale, rice and beans accented with pickled onions, fresh herbs and flavorful sauces. Bonus for the Hot Springs location - this hidden patio on the mountainside behind and above the restaurant.

210 Central Avenue, Hot Springs National Park * (501) 318-6054
917 North A Street, Fort Smith * (479) 573-0404
509 West Spring Street, Fayetteville * (479) 251-1650
RolandosRestaurant.com

89

CATFISH AND SALAD PLATE
The Shack

Right across Scenic Arkansas Highway Seven from Jessieville High School, this unassuming dairy diner serves up a remarkable plate of batter-light, perfectly seasoned catfish that's received high praise from visitors from all over the state. Order yours with the traditional sides of coleslaw, fries and hush puppies, or choose instead the recommendation of catfish with a side salad. The Ranch dressing is homemade.

7901 North Scenic Arkansas Highway 7, Jessieville
(501) 984-5619

90

CORNED BEEF HASH AND EGGS
Skyline Café

One of the oldest restaurants in western Arkansas, Skyline Café has served Mena and its surrounds since 1922. The crowd usually includes families, tourists and motorcycle enthusiasts, the latter of which come to ride the Talimena Scenic Byway. Here, the corned beef is shredded and hashed by hand, served hot with your eggs any way you want them. The pork chop breakfast is also highly recommended.

618 Mena Street, Mena
(479) 394-5152

91

BULL BURGER
The Smokin' Bull

Half a pound of well seasoned beef with your choice of cheese, plus lettuce, tomato, onion, and spicy-sweet pickles made right in the restaurant, with a swish of housemade "bull jam" on a fresh-baked bun (your choice of plain, cheese or jalapeño cheese) makes for one of the most incredible burgers you will ever tackle. Get yours with the beer battered Sidewinder fries.

306 South Elm Street, Emerson
(870) 547-2020 * Facebook.com/SmokinBullEmersonAR

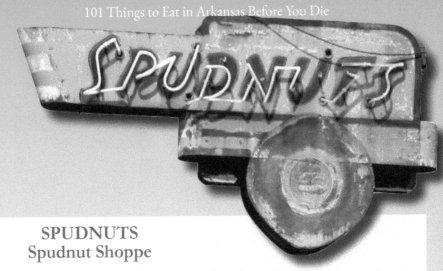

SPUDNUTS
Spudnut Shoppe

Al and Bob Pelton created the Spudnut, a potato flour doughnut, in Salt Lake City back in 1940. The franchise they sparked once claimed 600 locations across the United States - but a series of poor business deals left franchisees suddenly with no chain attachment in 1979. Most locations closed, but two shops in Lower Arkansas managed to survive. Of these, the Spudnut Shoppe in El Dorado retains its original neon and original recipe with these marvelous golden rounds served fresh and hot. Must be eaten within a few hours.

One other location, in Magnolia, sells Spudnuts in the morning and sandwiches and plate lunches at midday.

810 West Faulkner Street, El Dorado * (870) 863-9914

722 East Main Street, Magnolia * (870) 901-3636
Facebook.com/SpudnutShop

93

POT OF BEANS
Stubby's Hik'ry Pit Bar-B-Q

One of the smokiest creations known to modern Arkansas eaters, this bowl may appear simple, but it's arguably a small vessel with a large flavor. It's beans baked in sauce with bits of ham, placed at the bottom of a smoke pit, where the juices from hams, pork butts, brisket and chicken drip into the pot for a greater depth of seasoning. The pots are then topped with more smoked meats and sauce, making this the apex of barbecue power.

3024 Central Avenue, Hot Springs
(501) 624-1552 * StubbysBBQ.com

CATFISH AND CHICKEN DINNER
Wood's Place

The unofficial monument to Arkansas-created Grapette soda, this classic country get-together spot serves legendarily large fillets of catfish. It's all the little side notes - from the baskets of hush puppies and homemade rolls with butter and honey, to the green tomato pickle and tartar sauce, to the excellent Ranch fries, that add to this bastion of great Lower Arkansas edibles. The hand-pulled chicken tenders are also tasty. Get a Flywheel fried pie if you still have room when you're done. Take it with you if you're full as a tick.

1173 West Washington Street, Camden
(870) 836-0474 * WoodsPlace.com

CENTRAL

- [ ] Arthur's Prime Steakhouse, Little Rock
- [ ] Charlotte's Eats and Sweets, Keo
- [ ] Damgoode Pies, Little Rock/Fayetteville
- [ ] David Family Kitchen, Little Rock
- [ ] Eat My Catfish,
       Benton/Conway/Little Rock/North Litte Rock
- [ ] Franke's Cafeteria, Little Rock
- [ ] Heights Taco and Tamale Company, Little Rock
- [ ] Jimmy's Serious Sandwiches, Little Rock
- [ ] Lassis Inn, Little Rock
- [ ] Layla's Gyros and Pizzeria,
       Little Rock/North Little Rock
- [ ] Lindsey's Hospitality House, North Little Rock
- [ ] Loca Luna, Little Rock
- [ ] Lost Forty Brewing, Little Rock
- [ ] Mark's Do-Nuts, North Little Rock
- [ ] The Root Café, Little Rock
- [ ] Sim's Bar-B-Q, Little Rock
- [ ] Star of India, Little Rock
- [ ] Stoby's, Conway/Russellville
- [ ] Trio's Restaurant, Little Rock

ANY STEAK
Arthur's Prime Steakhouse

Jerry Barakat's hyper-focused attention to detail and dedication to providing Little Rock's premiere top-of-the-line executive atmosphere both shine within the lush marble-and-hardwood interior. Every steak receives that level of diligence, whether it's a T-bone, a Chicago-style bone-in ribeye, or the fantastic Prime Chateaubriand for Two, all handcut from high grade prime beef. Cuts of Australian wagyu and Kobe beef are also prized here.

16100 Chenal Parkway, Little Rock
(501) 821-1838 * ArthursPrimeSteakhouse.com

97

KEO KLASSIC and CARAMEL MERINGUE PIE
Charlotte's Eats and Sweets

Eaters come literally by the bus-loads to experience the ambrosial pies that come from Charlotte Bowl's ovens five days a week. It's not unusual to have to wait in line, even if you arrive before the eatery opens at 11 a.m. Coconut meringue is the one selected by *Southern Living* as the best such pie anywhere. The caramel meringue is an opulent delight. But you'd be remiss if you skipped the Keo Klassic - a sandwich of turkey, avocado, tomato, onion and Monterrey Jack cheese on sourdough bread, battered and fried in butter. Mercy.

290 Main Street, Keo
(501) 842-2123

THE ARTIE, STUFFY PINK
Damgoode Pies

Arkansas's answer to Chicago-style deep dish isn't deep, but it is thick, hearty and delectable. Damgoode offers four prime sauces - Original Red, Spicy White, Alfredo, and Pesto - and four blended sauces - Pink, Spicy Alfredo, Pesto Cream and Tomato Basil. The selections are a palate on which toppings shine. This particular creation, the Artie, is described as "A pie for the man who loves Artichokes. He should also like Mushrooms and Tomatoes, but just as friends." A perfect pizza for sharing. Also consider The Underdog, named to Food Network's *50 Slices for 50 States*, with its hamburger, red and yellow bell peppers, black olives and Cheddar cheese.

6706 Cantrell Road, Little Rock
2701 Kavanaugh Boulevard, Little Rock
500 President Clinton Avenue, Little Rock
(501) 664-2239
also 37 East Center Street, Fayetteville * (479) 444-7437
damgoodepies.com

OXTAILS
David Family Kitchen

The best soul food in the capital city, bar none. David Family Kitchen is open every day except Saturday, and has succulent fried chicken, which can be paired with waffles at breakfast or greens and yams at lunch. Rolls are lofty and cornbread is dense. On Thursdays, leave your shame at the door and suck marrows of these rich, savory oxtails. Grab extra napkins.

2301 Broadway Street, Little Rock
(501) 371-0141

BUCKET OF CRAWFISH BY THE POUND
Eat My Catfish

You would not be alone if you thought this group of catfish joints had been around for decades. There's a consistency to everything Eat My Catfish brings to the table. The multi-location fish place started out in 2008 as a food truck Travis Hester opened on his return from a career in finance in Dallas. Hester was just 24 when he set out to, as he put it, "sell catfish by the road." Today, his little start-up continues to grow. The catfish is good; for folks craving mudbugs, this is the place. Ask for them as spicy as you want them. This restaurant will oblige.

1205 Military Road, Benton * (501) 909-2323
10301 North Rodney Parham Road, Little Rock * (501) 222-8055
2125 Harkrider Street, Conway * (501) 588-1867
4216 East McCain Boulevard, North Little Rock * (501) 235-8667

EGGPLANT CASSEROLE
Franke's Cafeteria

Arkansas's oldest cafeteria and Central Arkansas's oldest restaurant continues to serve the classic dishes that have endured over the decades, including this dressing-style eggplant dish that has become synonymous with the restaurant. Filling, heartwarming and generously served, it's a particularly Arkansas flavor that seems perfect beside broiled chicken, roast beef or even as the star of its own vegetable plate.

11121 North Rodney Parham Road, Little Rock * (501) 225-4487
400 West Capitol Avenue, Little Rock * (501) 372-1919
1103 Fendley Drive, Conway * (501) 932-6123
FrankesCafeteria.com

PLATO 1947
Heights Taco and Tamale Company

For generations, Little Rock residents got their Ark-Mex fix at a Heights neighborhood restaurant called Browning's. After the restaurant closed, it was reopened as Heights Taco and Tamale Company in 2015 by the innovators at Yellow Rocket Concepts. The new menu focuses on Arkansas-style Mexican creations made from fresh ingredients such as tamales, enchiladas and a variety of tacos.

This throwback dish - a tribute to Browning's original Saltillo Plate - remains. The Plato 1947 includes a cheese enchilada with red sauce, an Arkansas Delta-style pork-filled tamale with chili and cheese, a hard shell ground beef taco, a guacamole-laden tostada, and two sides. Be sure to ask for the Melting Pot Cheese Dip, inspired by five of the greatest cheese dips in Little Rock.

5805 Kavanaugh Boulevard, Little Rock
(501) 313-4848 * Facebook.com/HeightsTaco

ARKANSAS FOOD HALL of FAME

FINALIST

THE GARDEN
Jimmy's Serious Sandwiches

The recipe for this epic meatless sandwich is posted on the wall right next to the door - but that doesn't keep customers from ordering up hundreds of The Garden sandwiches every single week. The perfect combination of spinach, alfalfa sprouts, mushrooms, cheeses, mayo, sunflower seeds and more on pumpernickel bread was created for the National Sandwich Competition in 1984 by Jimmy Weisman. One bite, and you'll understand why it won.

5116 West Markham Street, Little Rock
(501) 666-3354 * JimmysSeriousSandwiches.com

FRIED BUFFALO RIBS AND CATFISH
Lassis Inn

The exact opening date of this fish joint has been lost to time. Within this blue building south of Roosevelt Road, you'll encounter sign-borne admonitions not to dance. The lemonade is irresistably sweet, the green tomato pickle has a bite, and the hot plates that are brought to the table bear fillets and steaks of catfish and ribs of buffalo, a bottom-dwelling fish rarely found on any menu. If you want to try your hand at home, you can pick up batter to take with you. Cash only.

518 East 27th Street, Little Rock
(501) 372-8714

105

GYROS AND GREEK CALZONES
Layla's Gyros and Pizzeria

This humble Mediterranean hole in the wall has earned its sizable following, with consistently toothsome items added regularly. The Greek calzone filled with gyro meat and vegetables is so satisfying not just because of the thin, light dough and prodigious use of cheese, but because it's made with the excellent savory gyro meat prized by diners here. The basil cream pasta is a new, soon-to-be-favorite option as well.

9501 North Rodney Parham Road #7, Little Rock * (501) 227-7272
4546 East McCain Boulevard, North Little Rock *(501) 955-2300
LaylasGyros.com

SMOKED CHICKEN DINNER
Lindsey's Hospitality House

The Lindseys continue a tradition started in 1956 of offering some of the best smoked chicken, barbecue, fried chicken, hot links and fried catfish to be found in North Little Rock. The smoked chicken itself is lavishly moist and flavorful, falling right off the bone. Pair it with the so-very-sweet, syrupy yams - or save room for a piece of delightfully downhome sweet potato pie.

207 Curtis Sykes Drive, North Little Rock
(501) 374-5707 * LindseysBBQNMore.com

107

THE FIRST WHITE CHEESE DIP in AMERICA
Loca Luna

A boast well backed up, this is the original Mark Abernathy and Frank McGehee created in 1988, the one that set the stage for every other white cheese dip to come. The smooth blend of cheeses and spices with a crown of roasted corn is the yang to the traditional yellow dip's yin - warm, comforting, mellow. If tortilla chips aren't your speed, ask for housemade potato chips or pork cracklings for your indulgence.

3519 Old Cantrell Road, Little Rock
(501) 663-4666 * LocaLuna.com

RUSTIC MEAT PLATE with PORK BELLY
and a FLIGHT
Lost Forty Brewing

The brewery, named for a storied 40 acre plot of Lower Arkansas land somehow missed by the timber industry, has become synonymous with the growth of the Arkansas craft brew trend - a focused effort on small batch brewing, only sold within the borders of the state. The magnificent, continually shifting array of IPAs, stouts, bocks, blonds and such are worthy of a sampling most any time. The ace pairing of an eatery attached to the facility means the menu is tailored to fit the beverage. The Rustic Meat Plate, with its choice of pork belly, bratwurst or spicy jalapeño cheddar sausage alongside a molasses barbecue sauce, mustard made from the brewery's Rockhound IPA, housemade pickles and peppers, a selection of cheeses and fresh country bread from local favorite Old Mill Bread and Flour, is the perfect sharable for consuming beer with friends. The Turkey Reuben, a delightfully substantial sandwich, is also very worthy of note.

501 Byrd Street, Little Rock
(501) 319-7275 * Lost40Brewing.com

ARKANSAS
FOOD
HALL of FAME

FINALIST

109

DOUGHNUTS
Mark's Do-Nuts

Substantially biteworthy, yet surprisingly light. Meltingly wonderful. How these particular doughnuts manage to somehow be better than just about any other glazed doughnut you can find in Arkansas is a mystery, a sweet one, investigated and researched again and again by pastry lovers statewide. Whatever this little shop is doing, it does it well enough to draw flocks of customers every day it's open, always selling out.

4015 Camp Robinson Road, North Little Rock
(501) 753-2017 * Facebook.com/MarksDonutShop

110

CURRIED CHICKEN SALAD SANDWICH
The Root Café

Locally made bun. Locally raised chicken. Fresh herbs and spices. The Root Café's dedication to reducing food miles and bringing nearby produce, meats and breads to the table on its marvelous mismatched dishes is admirable. Its curried chicken salad, served with a fresh salad of super-local produce, is scrumptious. Fill your own Mason jar and bus your own table, and enjoy your afternoon respite at this beautiful reclaimed dairy bar on South Main.

1500 Main Street, Little Rock
(501) 414-0423 * TheRootCafe.com

PORK RIBS
Sim's Bar-B-Que

One of Little Rock's most distinctive flavors, Sim's thin, sweet and tangy sauce is identifiable not only on first taste, but the moment you wall through the door at any of the joint's three eateries. Take that sauce and drizzle it over fall-off-the-bone pork ribs, slap that meat on a piece of white bread, and you have heaven. Add in the sweet mustard potato salad, coleslaw, even a piece of sweet potato pie, and voila - there's a veritable feast of strong, urge-curbing flavors. The brisket and smoked bologna sandwiches are also potently addictive.

1307 John Barrow Road Suite A, Little Rock * (501) 224-2057
2415 Broadway Street, Little Rock * (501) 372-6868
7601 Geyer Springs Road, Little Rock * (501) 562-8844
SimsBBQAr.com

ARKANSAS
FOOD
HALL of FAME
HERITAGE

FINALIST

CHICKEN TIKKA KORMA
Star of India

"Welcome home!" isn't just a cliché at this longstanding favorite in West Little Rock. Sami Lal has been greeting customers, all of whom become immediate friends, to his establishment since 1993. They come back not only for the hospitality and utmost service, but for a thick menu of favorites from India, including a dozen breads, pages of curries and excellent biriyanis. The chicken tikka korma, with its spice-packed creamy sauce and succulent tandoori-roasted chicken, is as curative as it is tasty. Don't forget the kheer.

301 North Shackleford Road, Little Rock
(501) 227-9900 * LRStarOfIndia.com

ARKANSAS FOOD HALL of FAME

FINALIST

113

WHITE AND YELLOW CHEESE DIPS
Stoby's Restaurant

David and Patti Stobaugh's vaunted casual lunchrooms have long since earned their place as the go-to for college activities and gatherings, both for the University of Central Arkansas in Conway and for Arkansas Tech University in Russellville. It's the yellow cheese dip - with a thick, smooth texture unlike any other contender, that put the eateries on the map throughout the state. Recognition by hometown boy and *American Idol* winner Kris Allen put the dip in the national spotlight. The smooth, silky white has its own allure. Best get both.

805 Donaghey Avenue, Conway * (501) 327-5447
405 West Parkway Drive, Russellville * (479) 968-3816
Stobys.com

SHRIMP ENCHILADAS
Trio's Restaurant

Some folks thought Capi Peck was crazy to open her restaurant out on what was then the western edge of the city in 1986. But she, Brent Peterson and Stephanie Caruthers have kept this extraordinary Arkansas fusion restaurant going through the years. While the restaurant's late spring strawberry short-cake makes waves annually, and while its Peck Salad is considered one of the great heritage dishes of Arkansas's past, it's this simple but luxurious shrimp enchilada that gets the mention here. The soft tortilla filled with shrimp, the cream sauce, the choice of cheese, the fresh tomatoes and peppers - it's a perfectly constructed dish guaranteed to satiate and comfort. Do seek out the daily specials, all curated with care.

8201 Cantrell Road Suite 100, Little Rock
(501) 221-3330 * TriosRestaurant.com

ARKANSAS FOOD HALL of FAME

FINALIST

Index

This book would not be possible without the support of Arkansas's restaurant, hospitality and tourism industries, who work extraordinarily hard to ensure a good guest experience for visitors and locals alike.

Thank you to the Fort Smith Convention & Visitors Bureau, the Eureka Springs Advertising and Promotions Commission, the 1905 Basin Park Hotel, the West Memphis Convention & Visitors Bureau, Dogwood Hills Guest Farm, and King-Rhodes & Associates for assistance with lodging.

A special thanks to Kerry Kraus for proofreading this book.

And to Hunter Robinson and Grav Weldon, who were patient and helpful while I worked on tandem compiling this book and the next and who put up with me while I put this book in motion.

Kat Robinson is Arkansas's food historian and most enthusiastic road warrior. The Little Rock-based travel writer is the host of the Emmy-nominated documentary *Make Room For Pie: A Delicious Slice of The Natural State* and a committee member for the Arkansas Food Hall of Fame. The author of *Arkansas Food: The A to Z of Eating in The Natural State*, Robinson has also compiled the comprehensive travel guide for pie lovers, *Another Slice of Arkansas Pie: A Guide to the Best Restaurants, Bakeries, Truck Stops and Food Trucks for Delectable Bites in The Natural State* (2018). Her other books are *Arkansas Pie: A Delicious Slice of the Natural State* (2012), *Classic Eateries of the Ozarks and Arkansas River Valley* (2013), and *Classic Eateries of the Arkansas Delta* (2014). She is the Arkansas fellow and curator to the National Food and Beverage Foundation, and the 2011 Arkansas Department of Parks and Tourism Henry Award winner for Media Support. With *101 Things to Eat in Arkansas Before You Die*, Robinson provides a quick, succinct answer to the immediate question "where should I eat?"

Robinson's work appears in regional and national publications including *Food Network, Forbes Travel Guide, Serious Eats, AAA Magazines* and *AY Magazine*, among others. While she writes on food and travel subjects throughout the United States, she is best known for her ever-expanding knowledge of Arkansas food history and restaurant culture, all of which she explores on her 1200+ article website, *TieDyeTravels.com*. She lives with daughter Hunter and partner Grav Weldon in Little Rock.

For questions about Arkansas food or to reach the author, contact
kat@tiedyetravels.com.

For more information on this book and others through Tonti Press, visit
TontiPress.com.

CPSIA information can be obtained
at www.ICGtesting.com
Printed in the USA
LVHW071126180822
726273LV00007B/22